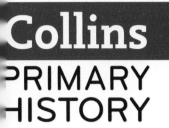

Collins
PRIMARY
HISTORY

Vi
Times

Pupil Book

Alf Wilkinson

William Collins' dream of knowledge for all began with the publication of his first book in 1819. A self-educated mill worker, he not only enriched millions of lives, but also founded a flourishing publishing house. Today, staying true to this spirit, Collins books are packed with inspiration, innovation and practical expertise. They place you at the centre of a world of possibility and give you exactly what you need to explore it.

Collins. Freedom to teach.

Published by Collins
An imprint of HarperCollins*Publishers*
The News Building
1 London Bridge Street
London
SE1 9GF

Browse the complete Collins catalogue at
www.collins.co.uk

© HarperCollins*Publishers* Limited 2019
Maps © Collins Bartholomew 2019

10 9 8 7 6 5 4 3 2 1

ISBN 978-0-00-831086-8

British Library Cataloguing-in-Publication Data
A catalogue record for this publication is available from the British Library.

Author: Alf Wilkinson
Publisher: Lizzie Catford
Product developer: Natasha Paul
Copyeditor: Sally Clifford
Indexer: Jouve India Private Ltd
Proofreader: Nikky Twyman
Image researcher: Alison Prior
Map designer: Gordon MacGilp
Cover designer and illustrator: Steve Evans
Internal designer: EMC Design
Typesetter: Jouve India Private Ltd
Production controller: Rachel Weaver
Printed and bound by Martins the Printers

MIX
Paper from responsible sources
FSC www.fsc.org   **FSC™ C007454**

This book is produced from independently certified FSC™ paper to ensure responsible forest management.

For more information visit:
www.harpercollins.co.uk/green

The publishers gratefully acknowledge the permission granted to reproduce the copyright material in this book. Every effort has been made to trace copyright holders and to obtain their permission for the use of copyright material. The publishers will gladly receive any information enabling them to rectify any error or omission at the first opportunity.

Contents

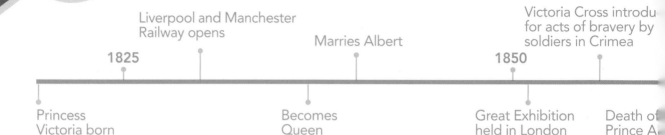

Liverpool and Manchester Railway opens

Marries Albert

Victoria Cross introdu[ced] for acts of bravery by soldiers in Crimea

1825

1850

Princess Victoria born

Becomes Queen

Great Exhibition held in London

Death of Prince A[lbert]

Victoria and Albert

Victoria was born in 1819, in Kensington Palace, London. She did not expect to rule – she was fifth in line to the throne – but in 1837, at the age of 18, she became Queen. She continued to rule until her death in 1901. In 1840, she married her cousin Albert, a German prince. They were very much in love, and had nine children, although Queen Victoria hated being pregnant and was a very strict mother. She was very short, only 1.5 metres tall, but when she was young she was very attractive. The Royal couple were very popular. Over 400,000 visitors came to London for Victoria's **coronation**. She was the first monarch to live in Buckingham Palace, and the first to use the new anaesthetic chloroform, while giving birth to her son Leopold in 1853.

Queen Victoria and her family, painted in 1846

Victoria had a very unhappy childhood, totally controlled by her mother, so was determined to do things her way. She was in control. For example, she threatened to **abdicate** several times when she could not persuade her prime minister, who ran the Government, to do exactly as she wanted! There were at least six attempts to **assassinate** her.

Death of Albert

Albert died in 1861, probably from typhoid carried in the bad drains of Buckingham Palace. Victoria was devastated. She mourned Albert for the rest of her life. She refused to carry out *any* royal engagements for many years.

Becomes empress
of India

1875

Golden Jubilee
celebrations

Diamond Jubilee
celebrations

Boer
War

Death of
Victoria

1900

Jubilee

In 1887, Victoria celebrated her Golden Jubilee. Over 50 kings and princes from around the world were invited to London to join the celebrations. The event showed how powerful Britain had become while Victoria was Queen. The Queen's Diamond Jubilee procession on 22 June 1897 followed a route 10 kilometres long through London and included troops from all over the **empire**. There were vast crowds of spectators. After the Jubilee, she became increasingly unwell, and died in January 1901 at one of her favourite places – Osborne House. Because many of her children married into the royal families of Europe, she became known as 'the grandmother of Europe'.

> Queen Victoria wore nothing but black after her husband Albert died in 1861.

Queen Victoria towards the end of her life

Think about it!

1. Why do you think the young Queen Victoria and Prince Albert were so popular?
2. Which of these two pictures on this spread do you think is most useful for us in finding out about Queen Victoria? Why?

Let's do it!

1. Research the life of Prince Albert. What do his actions tell us about Victorian times? How much influence did Albert have over Victoria?
2. Find out about mourning in Victorian times. How long did people usually wear black for? How typical was Queen Victoria in her mourning for Albert?

Key words

coronation

abdicate

assassinate

empire

Inside the Great Exhibition

The Crystal Palace

In 1848, it was decided to hold a 'Great Exhibition' to highlight Britain's new industrial wealth. Prince Albert was heavily involved in the process. A competition was held to design a building. There were over 240 entries, but no one won! In the end Joseph Paxton was asked to design and build his Crystal Palace. It was 562 metres long and 124 metres wide. It was **prefabricated**, and used 300,000 sheets of glass. Over 5000 **navvies** were employed building it. It had to be built around a huge tree after MPs complained about chopping it down!

The Great Exhibition

The exhibition contained 100,000 exhibits, about half from Britain and the rest from across the whole world. Inventions like the electric telegraph were on show, as was the Koh-i-Noor diamond – at the time, the biggest in the world. One of the strangest exhibits was a folding piano, suitable for sailors to use on their yachts. The exhibition was supposed to show off Britain's industrial expertise. Instead, new agricultural machines from America, precision engineering from Germany, and watches from Switzerland grabbed much of the attention of visitors.

Visitors

The Exhibition ran from May to October and in that time over 6 million tickets were sold. On the opening day admission was £1. Then until 22 May, it cost 5 shillings (25p) to get in; after that, it was 1 shilling (5p) except on Fridays, when it cost 2 shillings and 6 pence (12.5p) and Saturdays, when the price was 5 shillings (25p) The different prices were designed to keep rich and poor people separate. One old lady walked all the way from Penzance, in Cornwall, to London to see the Great Exhibition. Thomas Cook ran special excursion trains to London. One, from York, cost only 5 shillings (25p) return. (As a comparison, typical worker's wage at this time was about 16 shillings, or 80p, per week.)

▲ *The Great Exhibition 1851 in Hyde Park, London*

Profits

By October 1851, the Great Exhibition had made a profit of £186,000. This was enough money to buy land in South Kensington and build the museums that stand there today, as well as the Royal Albert Hall. Many of the exhibits formed the first collections of the Victoria and Albert Museum and can still be seen there today. The Crystal Palace was moved to South London, where it remained in use until it burned down in 1936. The Great Exhibition is a perfect symbol of the Victorian age – **innovation** in industry, confidence and wealth, and trading with countries across the world.

Think about it!

1. Why do you think Joseph Paxton's building became known as the Crystal Palace?
2. What do the admission prices for the Great Exhibition tell us about Victorian Britain?
3. Do you think the Great Exhibition was a success? Why?

Let's do it!

1. Find out about the exhibits on show in the Great Exhibition. What do they tell us about Victorian times?
2. Read old newspaper accounts of visiting the Exhibition. Write a diary entry of a visit you might have made to the Exhibition. What would you go to see?

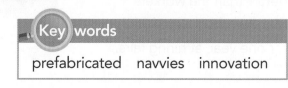

Key words

prefabricated   navvies   innovation

When Queen Victoria was born in 1819, around 75 per cent of Britain's population lived in the countryside. Perhaps 50 per cent worked in farming. There were still some traditional open-field villages dating back to the Middle Ages, where every field was divided into strips, with each farmer working strips in each field. People worked **communally**, so everyone had to grow the same crops and harvest them at the same time.

Wages were low. In some areas in the south of England, men earned 8 shillings (40p) a week, perhaps a little more at harvest time. This meant that food was in short supply – many labourers rarely ate any meat at all, unless they could **poach** a rabbit from the woods. As wages were so bad, people could not afford to pay much rent, so housing was bad. Most people lived on bread and cheese, with the odd bit of meat and any vegetables they could grow. Sugar and tea were very expensive, because there was a big tax on imports. In 1830, for example, the tax on tea was 100 per cent!

People depended on their gardens to keep them in vegetables and fruit throughout the year.

Child labour

Children worked too – very few went to school for long enough to learn to read. Picking up stones, chasing away birds and helping with the harvest were tiring jobs that might earn a child 6d (2.5p) a week, but every little helped, especially when it came to finding the money for a new pair of boots. Most children wore hand-me-down clothes.

There was little or no **mechanisation**, so most jobs were done by hand. Harvesting, for example, was done using a scythe or sickle, which was back-breaking work. Horses pulled the ploughs and the carts, and were probably treated much better than the workers. Many workers were hired for one year, at hiring fairs.

Inside a farm labourer's cottage, Dorchester, 1846

Harvest time

Once hired, they would **live in** for the year, get board plus lodging, plus a small sum of money at the end of the year.

The domestic system

In some areas, women also spun wool into yarn, and some people – mostly men – would weave the yarn into woollen cloth. Merchants would come to the village bringing wool, and return later to collect the cloth. This brought in extra money, especially in the winter.

Think about it!

1. Do you think *everybody* in the countryside was poor?
2. What would it be like living in a house like the one shown in the image on page 8?
3. Why do you think horses were treated better than workers?

Let's do it!

1. Find out what crops were grown on Victorian farms, and which animals were kept.
2. Research the **domestic system**. How did it work?
3. Would you have enjoyed living in the countryside in Victorian times?

 Key words

communally   poach   mechanisation   live in   domestic system

Change... for the better?

Increasing demand

Between 1801 (when the first **census** was held) and 1871, the population of Britain doubled to 21 million people. More people meant more demand for food. The railways meant that food could be carried and sold over a much wider area, so it was a good time to own a farm. The remaining open fields were made into separate farms. The cost of hedges and ditches meant many small farmers lost their land and became labourers. However, this did mean that farmers could grow what they wanted when they wanted. However, labourers' wages stayed low.

In 1850, 100,000 tonnes of guano – dried bird poo – was imported from Chile to use as fertiliser on British farms.

Changes in farming practice

New crops were grown, including turnips and clover, which were used to feed animals. This meant there were more animals. More animals meant more manure on the fields, and this in turn meant better crops. Fields were drained using mass-produced clay pipes. Animals were improved by selective breeding. Sheep were now bred for meat rather than wool. Prize winning animals were sold for thousands of pounds. New farmyards were built, incorporating the latest technology. Mixed farming benefited both animals and crops.

New machines

New machines, like McCormick's reaper, made harvesting much easier, and steam power came to the farm. Ploughs, threshing machines and wood saws could all be powered by **traction engines** that travelled from farm to farm. It was a good time to be a farmer–high prices and high rents, and easy money to borrow to buy new machinery.

An 1887 illustration of a McCormick mechanical reaper – similar to those that were on show at the Great Exhibition

Steam-powered threshing machines, run from a traction engine (like this one), speeded up the job. However, they put many men out of work in autumn and winter after the harvest

Some jobs were still done by hand. This 1857 print shows maids milking cows

Changing times

In the 1880s, farmers faced competition from imported food from abroad – wheat from the USA, canned and frozen beef from South America and Australia, lamb from New Zealand and butter from Denmark. These goods were all cheaper than British-grown food. Some farmers went bankrupt. Others changed to growing vegetables and fruit for the people in the new towns, or selling milk and cheese. Once again, it was hard times for farming.

Think about it!

1. What was the impact of steam power on farming?
2. Were all jobs done by steam power?
3. Why did imported food make life harder for farmers?

Let's do it!

1. Use the pictures from Unit 2.1 and 2.2 to describe how working on a farm changed during Victorian times. Which, in your opinion, was the biggest change?
2. Have some things on the farm stayed the same?
3. Was it better to be a farmer at the beginning of Queen Victoria's reign, or at the end of it?

Key words

census   traction engines

The Poor Law

Ever since the time of Elizabeth I, each parish or town had to look after its poor people. In Victorian times, as the population increased and labourers' wages fell, there were more and more poor people to look after. Wealthy people didn't like paying for this, so the Government passed the Poor Law Amendment Act in 1834. Each town or group of villages had to build a workhouse. If poor people wanted help, they had to go and live in the workhouse, where they had to work for their keep. Conditions were bad. Men were separated from women, and meals were mostly **broth**. In 1845, there was a riot in Andover Workhouse, where people crushing bones to use as fertiliser were fighting over the bone marrow so they could eat it!

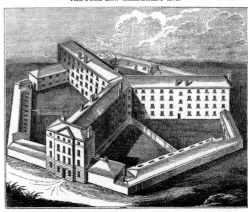

The Mirror
OF
LITERATURE, AMUSEMENT, AND INSTRUCTION.

No. 765.]   SATURDAY, FEBRUARY 27, 1836.   [PRICE 2d.

THE POOR LAW AMENDMENT ACT.

ABINGDON NEW WORKHOUSE.

The new workhouse in Abingdon, 1836

Protest

When people tried to protest about their conditions harsh laws were used against them. In Tolpuddle,

Four of the Tolpuddle Martyrs, convicted in 1834

Dorset, six farm labourers tried to get their wages increased from six shillings a week (30p). Their wages had been cut three years in a row. They were arrested and put on trial. When they were found guilty, they were **transported** to Australia for seven years. All they had tried to do was to form a **trade union** to get better wages. Rich landowners didn't want to pay higher wages, so the Tolpuddle Martyrs, as they became known, were used as an example to stop other people from protesting.

Going to live somewhere else

Many people, especially younger and more skilled workers, left the countryside to go and live in the towns and work in the new factories (see Unit 3). Wages were better there. Of course, the new factories made life worse in the countryside. Those spinning and weaving under the domestic system lost their jobs, because new factory cloth was much cheaper.

Thousands **emigrated** to other countries, like Canada, USA, Australia and New Zealand. Some parishes paid for unemployed workers to go abroad, as it was cheaper than keeping them in the workhouse. Some countries offered cheap or free passage to encourage workers to go and live there. Many emigrants were able to make a new life in these countries. Sometimes they wrote home encouraging others from their village to join them.

> *Australia and New Zealand offered free passages, to encourage farm workers to go and live there.*

Think about it!

1. Why did the Government set up workhouses for poor people?
2. How much did it cost to go to Australia if you were an agricultural labourer?
3. Why do you think the law was so harsh on the Tolpuddle Martyrs? What does that tell us about living in the Victorian countryside?

Let's do it!

1. Find out what it was like living in the workhouse.
2. Research what happened to the Tolpuddle Martyrs after they were found guilty.
3. What was life like for emigrants?

Key words

broth
transported
trade union
emigrated

Towns and cities in Victorian Britain grew very rapidly. Manchester, for example, had 90,000 people in 1801 and 544,000 when Queen Victoria died 100 years later. There were no town planning laws, so factories and houses were built close together. Builders would squeeze as many houses on a plot as they could. There was often no running water, and there might be one toilet in the yard for 100 houses. There were no rubbish collections, either, so rubbish piled up in the streets and yards. So many people needed somewhere to live that most people shared houses.

Often a family of 10 or more had to live in one room!

Disease

Living like this meant it was difficult to keep clean and tidy. Wages were low so people were often under nourished. Lots of children died before they reached the age of five. Cholera, typhoid, measles, chickenpox and tuberculosis were all killer diseases, and there were few doctors. Doctors knew little about the causes of disease, even if the sick could afford one.

Year	UK deaths from cholera
1831/2	50,000
1848	60,000
1854	20,000

Some people lived better. Skilled workers, for example, earned higher wages and could afford houses for their families. Richer people often paid to have running water installed in their homes, and towards the end of the century **water closets** became increasingly popular. Some towns built public baths so people could pay to have a wash or a bath.

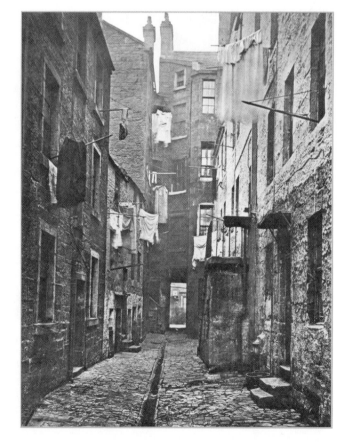

A court of houses, in Glasgow, photographed in the 1860s. How did they dry their washing?

Advert for Pears' Soap, 1893

Edward Street, Saltaire, Yorkshire, photographed in 2017. How can you tell this is a modern photograph?

Were all towns the same?

Some people were very concerned about how their workers lived. The chocolate-producing Cadbury brothers, for example, moved their factory out of the middle of Birmingham and built a town, called Bournville, for their workers. The owner of Pears' Soap, Lever Brothers, built a town called Port Sunlight. Titus Salt, a cloth manufacturer in Bradford, built the town of Saltaire for his workers. People in these towns were lucky to have a much nicer place to live. Gradually, laws were passed by the Government that made improvements in houses and sanitation. Therefore, by the time Victoria died, many people lived in better conditions.

Think about it!

1. Were living conditions bad in the towns and cities?
2. Which of the houses would you have preferred to live in – the one in Glasgow or the one in Saltaire? Why?
3. Why do you think Pears' Soap used children covered in dirt to advertise its product?

Let's do it!

1. Look at the image of the court of houses in Glasgow in the 1860s. Make a list of all the health hazards you can see.
2. Find out about living in the towns and cities. Why were conditions so bad?
3. Were conditions bad for everybody?
4. Research the killer diseases of Victorian England. What caused them? How were they treated?

Key word

water closets

Working in the new factories

At this time, England became known as the 'workshop of the world', because of the new factories producing cotton and woollen cloth. These huge buildings employed thousands of workers – men, women and children.

In the new factories, men, women and children often worked 14 hours a day, six days a week.

Steam-powered machines could, if necessary, run 24 hours a day. It was hot, dusty, noisy and dangerous work, and accidents were common. There was no **compensation** if you were injured and could no longer work. Children as young as seven or eight would be made to crawl under the moving machines to keep them running. Cotton cloth was sold all over the world.

Other types of work

There was plenty of other work too. Steam power needed lots of coal, so coal mines employed many people. Iron and steel production grew. All these people in towns needed food, so there was more work in shops. As there were no fridges or freezers, people would shop for food every day, usually in the evening after work. Shop workers' hours were very long. People who could read and write sometimes worked as clerks in offices. There were no computers or typewriters, so everything had to be written out by hand, including copies of documents. Children had to work to bring in some money for the family budget. Young boys sometimes worked as chimney sweeps. They would have to climb up inside a chimney, which was sometimes still hot, and sweep the soot off the inside.

▲ *Cotton factory in Saltaire, Yorkshire, c1880*

Uncertain hours of work

Much of the work was **irregular**. For example, thousands of workers would turn up at London docks every morning at 6:00 a.m. and wait to see if they had any work that day, loading or unloading ships. They only got paid if they worked. If a factory ran out

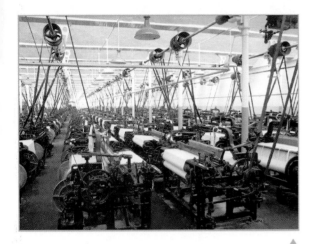

Inside Queen Street Mill,
Burnley Lancashire, as it is today

of orders, or the raw cotton was late in arriving from America, all the workers would be told not to come back until there was work for them. It was uncertain – workers never knew how much money they might earn from one week to the next. That made budgeting for rent and food very difficult indeed.

Young boy employed
as a chimney sweep

Think about it!

1. What would it be like working in a cotton factory, like the ones in the pictures? Would it be better if you were a skilled man running the steam engine or a young child watching the machines?

2. Where would you rather work – a cotton factory, a farm or as a chimney sweep? Why?

Let's do it!

1. Why were working conditions in the new factories so bad?

2. Find out how much factory workers earned. Was it more or less than farm labourers?

3. Imagine you live in a house next to the cotton mill above. Describe what you might see, hear and do in a typical day.

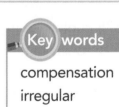

Key words

compensation
irregular

Self-help

In the 19th century, most people believed that if you were poor it was your own fault. You must have spent your money on immoral things instead of food or saving for the future. Samuel Smiles published a best-selling book on the subject in 1859. Some people tried hard to improve their own lives.

Some people in Rochdale, Lancashire, set up a cooperative shop in 1844. They owned the shop, and kept prices low and fair. They shared the profits. They also made sure that the foods they sold were **unadulterated**. Other examples of self-help were: building societies, where people saved up until they had enough to buy their own house; and burial societies, where people paid 1d per week so they would have enough money to pay for their funeral.

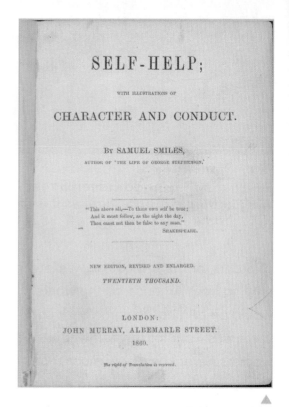

Samuel Smiles 'Self-Help', published in 1859

Government help

Increasingly, some people felt that self-help was not enough. Government would have to intervene. Slowly the Government was persuaded to do something. In the 1830s and 1840s, Parliament passed **acts** to control working in factories and coal mines, and to build houses. The 1848 and 1875 Public Health Acts made councils improve drains and sewers, to make towns better places to live in. Slowly things were getting better.

Shopkeepers often mixed dust with tea, or chalk with flour, in order to make more money.

Women's rights

In Victorian times, women had very few rights. Their father (and then their husband) controlled their money, their children and their education. Some women thought this was very unfair, and began to demand changes. Caroline Norton was one of these women.

She played a large part in getting new laws passed that gave women much more control over their own lives.

Caroline Norton, campaigner for women's rights

Lord Shaftesbury – the greatest reformer of them all?

Social reform

Many other people worked for change. Dr Barnardo set up schools and homes for homeless children, Seebohm Rowntree investigated poverty in York, Florence Nightingale made hospitals safer. But perhaps the most important reformer was Lord Shaftesbury, who spent his whole life demanding improvements in factories, in coal mines, in schools, in stopping young boys working as chimney sweeps, and much more. One of his **biographers** wrote, 'No man has in fact ever done more to lessen the extent of human misery or to add to the sum total of human happiness.'

Think about it!

1. What did most to improve people's lives: self-help, social reformers, or the Government?
2. Why might adulterated foods be dangerous to eat?
3. Was town life better in 1901 than it was in 1837?

Let's do it!

1. Research some of the reformers mentioned on these pages. How did they make people's lives better?
2. Find out about the Public Health Act of 1875. How did it improve life in the towns and cities?
3. Why might the Government be reluctant to act to make things better?

Key words

unadulterated
acts
biographers

On 15 September 1830, the first train ran on the Liverpool and Manchester Railway. Things would never be the same again. Previously, people and post travelled by stagecoach, which was expensive and slow. Before, goods travelled by river and canal, which was even slower and still expensive.

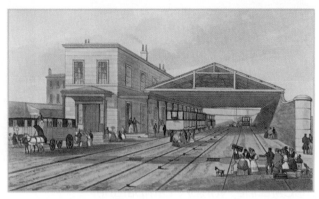

The railway station in Liverpool, 1830

The Liverpool and Manchester Railway was the first to be powered solely by steam engines and was, in effect, a proper railway. The Stockton and Darlington Railway (opened in 1825), for instance, used horses to pull its passenger coaches, and used a **stationary engine** to pull coal trains up a steep hill. The railway was so successful that, by 1872, there were 25,500 kilometres of railway in Britain. Every town and village wanted their own railway!

Early railways made their money carrying coal, and first-class passengers (that is, wealthy people). But it wasn't long before they realised they could make money carrying ordinary people in third-class carriages. By 1875, the railways were carrying over 450 million passengers each year.

Workmen wait to get the train to work in London, October 1884

Impact of the railway

Everything was so much faster! By the 1890s, trains were regularly running at 110 kilometres per hour or more. Before the railway, 16 kilometres an hour in a coach was fast, and most ordinary people walked everywhere. In 1745, it took

two weeks to travel by coach from London to Edinburgh. However, by 1901, you could do it in nine hours by train.

Railways created thousands of jobs – either building or running the railway. New towns like Swindon and Crewe grew up, building railway engines and all the equipment a railway needed. Thomas Cook, as we saw in Unit 1.2, started running holiday excursions, and not just to the Great Exhibition.

People could live further away from where they worked, either in new **suburbs** or in **commuter** towns. People could eat better, because food reached the towns and cities more quickly, making it cheaper and fresher.

Finally, the railways led to the growth of seaside resorts, like Margate, Skegness and Blackpool. People could quickly travel to spend time at the sea. The seaside holiday was born!

A trip to the seaside. Can you spot all the entertainment on the beach?

Railways led to the growth of seaside resorts in England. It was now cheap and quick to get to the sea!

Railway time

Perhaps one of the most interesting effects of the railway was 'railway time'. Time used to be set in England by the rising and setting on the sun which, in Cornwall, might be 10 minutes earlier or later than in London. People quickly realised that, to run a railway, everyone needed to use the same time. This is when time across the whole country was standardised.

Think about it!

1. How similar are the railway stations in 1830 and 1884? How similar are they both to stations today?
2. How similar is the Victorian seaside to the seaside today?

Let's do it!

1. Do you agree that the railway 'changes everything'?
2. What would you say was the main impact of the railway?

Key words

stationary engine

suburbs

commuter

As an island nation, Britain depended on its navy to protect it from invasion. It also needed a **merchant navy** to import and export goods. Britain's wealth depended on the sea.

The coal trade

For centuries, coal from north east England had been loaded onto collier ships at ports like Blyth. These would then sail south, mostly to London, delivering the coal. In fact, London called its coal 'sea coal', because it arrived by sea. Captain Cook used one of these collier ships to sail to the Pacific Ocean on his voyages of discovery in the late 18th century.

Wood and sail

At the start of Queen Victoria's reign, most ships were made of wood and powered by sail. There were small ships like the colliers and **coasters** that travelled from port to port, across the English Channel (in fact, wherever they could find a cargo). But there were also much larger ones, which travelled the world. It took around 32 days to sail across the Atlantic to America, or six months to sail to India or Australia. A special type of ship was designed for the tea trade from China, Ceylon (now Sri Lanka) and India. These, like the *Cutty Sark*, were **clippers**: long, narrow, with lots of sail, and designed for speed. The first cargoes of

Loading coal ships, Sunderland, around 1895

Australian stamp showing the tea clipper Cutty Sark *in full sail; stamp issued in 1984. You can still see the* Cutty Sark *in London*

tea to London made the most money, so each year there was a race to be first home.

Iron and steam

Isambard Kingdom Brunel was the engineer who built the Great Western Railway from London to Bristol. He had a vision of a railway all the way to America. He designed several ships, including the SS *Great Britain*, to carry passengers in style across the Atlantic. A steamship like this could reach New York in 10 days! The SS *Great Britain* was new. It was made of iron, powered by steam-driven propellers, but it still carried emergency sails. Later ships quickly did away with the sails.

Launch of the SS *Great Britain* in 1843. You can still see SS *Great Britain* in Bristol Docks

Which was better – a sailing ship or a steamship?

Think about it!

1. How did the design of ships change in Victorian times?
2. Why were ships so important to Britain?
3. Why do you think so many people were at the launch of SS *Great Britain*?

Let's do it!

1. The Suez Canal was opened in 1869. What impact did its opening have on travel by sea?
2. Research either the *Cutty Sark* or SS *Great Britain*. What was so new about their designs?
3. How different are the ships shown in this unit?

Key words

merchant navy   coaster   clippers

23

Horses, horses everywhere...

Whether people lived in towns or the countryside, they depended on horses. Rich people kept horses for riding and had a carriage or two as well, so they needed stables and servants, including a carriage driver, to look after all these horses. In towns, people used horse taxis and buses of all descriptions to get around. This one, owned by the London and North Western Railway, was used to take first-class passengers from the station to where they were going.

Travelling by bus, Victorian style. Notice the push bikes on the roof!

Children could earn a penny sweeping the street. So someone could cross the road without getting their shoes and clothes dirty or smelly!

Streets were full of delivery carts, like the one below. Cattle and sheep, ducks and geese, were walked to the butcher's to be slaughtered, but everything else had to be carried by hand or was delivered by cart. Every street was covered in horse droppings.

Trams and trolley buses

From the 1860s, people began to use horse-drawn trams. Later, around 1900, electric-powered trams were developed. These were usually supplied from overhead cables and ran on rails laid in the middle of the street. The routes were expensive to build, but could carry people quickly and cheaply across towns. Soon, every town

Delivering food to the shops

and city wanted its own electric trams and trolley buses. It meant that people no longer had to live right next to where they worked, or no longer had to walk several kilometres each day to and from work. These changes made huge differences to life in Victorian towns and cities.

Electric tram in London, about 1907

London underground

The first underground railway in the world opened in 1863. It ran under the streets of London. Carriages were lit by gas and the trains were pulled by steam locomotives. It was all very noisy and dirty! The first electric train arrived in 1890. Soon, underground lines reached out into the countryside and commuters could easily travel from there into the middle of London to work. Land around London began to be built on, and houses near an underground station were very popular indeed.

Think about it!

1. Why were there so many horses in Victorian times?
2. Why were electric trams and trolley buses so much better?
3. Why could people now live further away from where they worked?

Let's do it!

1. Imagine living in a town or city in the 1870s. Describe what you might see, hear and smell as you make your way to work. How similar, and how different, would your journey to work be today?
2. Research all the different kinds of horse-drawn vehicles you might find in a Victorian town or city. Why were there so many different types of vehicle?
3. How did travelling change while Queen Victoria was alive?

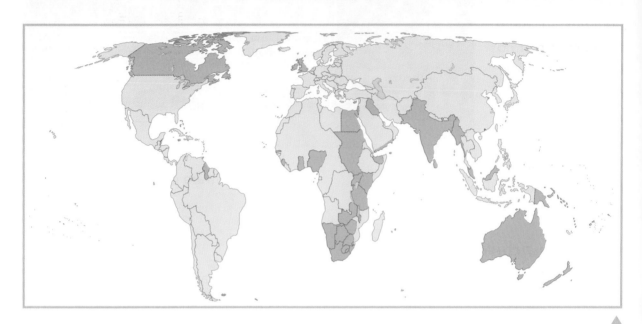

The British Empire at its peak in 1921

By 1900, Britain ruled an empire of 450 million people, covering 56 different colonies around the world in 1921, at its peak. People said that the sun never set on the British Empire. From looking at the map on the right, can you work out why they said this?

Political power

At the time, people thought you needed an empire to be a superpower. Britain kept some places for protection – Gibraltar, for example, was a huge navy base at the entrance to the Mediterranean Sea. Similarly, South Africa protected the trade route into the Indian Ocean.

Having an empire made a country rich and powerful.

Trade

Britain needed to import food and raw materials – foods like frozen meat and butter from Australia and New Zealand, and wheat from Canada. Cotton from Egypt kept the textile factories in England busy, rubber was imported from Malaysia and palm oil from West Africa was used in making margarine and soap. The colonies were also an important market for British goods – textiles, coal, iron and steel, for example.

Emigration

As we have already seen (Unit 2.3) many people in Britain were poor. Politicians argued that Britain had 'surplus' people. People were encouraged to emigrate to colonies like Canada and Australia, and could sometimes even travel there for free.

Discovery and exploration

Much of the continent of Africa was unknown to Europeans in 1850. Exploration societies were set up to fill in the gaps on the map. One of the most famous was John Speke, who tried to find the source of the River Nile. Mary Kingsley explored West Africa in the 1890s. Successful explorers became famous in Britain – everyone wanted to read and hear about their travels.

▲ Scottish missionary Mary Slessor in what is now Nigeria

Missionaries

Many people at the time thought non-whites were inferior to whites, and that they needed to be taught to be better people. They also thought that they should spread Christianity. **Missionaries** like Mary Slessor spent years in faraway places trying to turn people into Christians, to dress like Europeans and to open schools and colleges. They talked of it as the 'white man's burden'. Most of them thought they were helping people have a better life.

Think about it!

1. Which of the reasons for having an empire
   a. do you think were most important?
   b. *people at the time* thought were most important? Why?
2. Do you think Mary Slessor was a good person?
3. In what ways have attitudes changed since 1850?

Key word

missionaries

Let's do it!

1. Compare a map of Africa in 1850 with a map of Africa in 1900. How did the map change in that time?
2. How similar is the map of Africa in 1900 to the map of Africa today?
3. Find out about famous explorers in Africa. Why did they go to Africa?

British India in Victorian Times

The British East India Company started trading with India in the time of Queen Elizabeth I. Britain wanted India's silk, spices, jute, cotton, tea and coffee. It sold textiles, coal, iron and steel to India. Gradually Britain gained more and more control over India until, by the time of Queen Victoria, Britain ruled most of India. Around 40,000 British officials ran the whole country. They lived a luxurious lifestyle, with lots of servants and summer houses in the hills at places like Simla, to avoid the heat of the plains. They lived in a way they could never have afforded in Britain.

Revolt or mutiny?

Britain's army in India was made up of British soldiers (mostly officers) and Indian **sepoys**. Some were treated well by the British, and some not so well. In 1857, a huge revolt broke out among many of the Indian troops, complaining about harsh British rule, although some remained on the side of the British. No one knows exactly how many died in the fighting, or in the **reprisals** afterwards. British women and children were killed by the mutineers, and the British wanted revenge.

Historical interpretations

Historians have written lots about the events of 1857, and what they say often depends on where and when they lived. If you are pro-British, then 1857 is often seen as a mutiny or rebellion again British rule. If you are pro-Indian, then 1857 is seen as a war of independence, the first attempt to win India back from the British.

Siege of Lucknow, 1857

Victoria railway station, Mumbai, opened in 1888, now known as Chhatrapati Shivaji Terminus railway station, after an emperor from the 17th century

After 1857

Some people argue that Britain was good for India. Canals and railways were built, farms were irrigated and European-style education was introduced. People learned to play cricket. English became the language of government and business. The British built 3700 kilometres of roads and 4600 kilometres of railways, opened 2900 schools and increased the area of farmland from 1620 square kilometres to 13,000 square kilometres. When Queen Victoria came to the throne, there were no hospitals in India, but by 1900 there were 65.

Think about it!

1. Why do historians have different names for events in India in 1857?

2. Do you think it matters what the events of 1857 are called?

3. In your opinion, was being a British **colony** good for India?

Key words

sepoys
reprisals
colony

Let's do it!

1. Research life for the British in India in Victorian times.
2. Find out about events in India in 1857. What would *you* call the event?
3. Research the Rani of Jhansi and the part she played in 1857.
4. Why do you think the British called India the 'jewel in the crown'?
5. Find out why most Indians in the 20th century wanted the British out of India.

Was the British Empire a good thing?

Pax Britannica

In many colonies Britain brought peace and order, an end to fighting between different peoples. Britain's leaders referred to this as 'Pax Britannica' – peace brought to the area by Britain, its armed forces and its administrators. However, many people in the colonies didn't want Britain and its peace. They wanted to be left alone and to run their own affairs.

The shortest war in history – Zanzibar, 1896

For Britain?

Having such a huge empire made Britain very powerful and influential in the world. Other countries were sometimes scared by the size of Britain's armed forces, especially its navy. Few countries dared to oppose Britain, and small countries especially were easy to defeat. For example, in 1896, Zanzibar in East Africa was defeated in a war lasting 38 minutes! Britain thought the new ruler of Zanzibar was too pro-German, so insisted he was replaced. When he refused, the Royal Navy bombarded the palace until the Sultan fled.

Trading with the colonies made Britain wealthy, as we have already seen. The colonies had to send their goods to Britain, and buy British goods in return. Having an empire made Britain wealthy as well as powerful.

For the colonies?

As we have seen in India, Britain built new ports, connected to railways and canals, to transport goods back to Britain. But the routes were always to the coast, for overseas trade. Schools were built educating people to work in the administration of the colonies, although these people weren't given too much power. Natives were

Who benefited most from the Empire – Britain or the colonies?

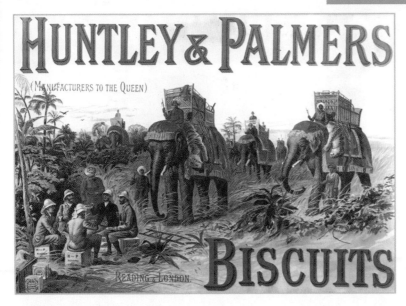

◄ *An advert for Huntley & Palmers biscuits, 1894*

regarded as cheap labour to be exploited. Prices were fixed in Britain's favour rather than in favour of the colonies – everything seemed to be for Britain, and not the colonies. Any opposition was treated harshly, as in Zanzibar.

What do historians say about the British Empire?

Professor Niall Ferguson says that Britain put lots of money into developing the economies of Africa and India. Modern technology like the telegraph increased as the British Empire grew. He also argues that British rule was usually honest, which is uncommon in empires.

Professor Simon Schama argues that the British Empire was based on a lie. He believes that the British talked about freedom, good government and free trade without actually doing it. They took most of the profits, not allowing the majority of the people in the Empire any benefits.

Think about it!

1. What do you think Huntley & Palmers thought about the British Empire?
2. How do the two historians disagree about the British Empire?

Let's do it!

1. Draw up a balance sheet of the British Empire, with all the good things on one side and all the bad things on another. Which list is longer?
2. Why do historians disagree about the British Empire?

Most Victorians worked very long hours for low wages, and had little money to spare for entertainment. The Bank Holiday Act 1871 introduced four paid holidays for all workers (five in Scotland), but that was all the holidays many people got.

Hotel Metropole, Blackpool, c1890–1910

For richer people, it was different. They went to the theatre or to dining clubs. Or they visited places like Madame Tussauds in London, or the zoo (for a ride on an elephant or to see the lions being fed). They held musical evenings and concerts in their own homes, with singers grouped around a piano. They enjoyed a seaside holiday staying in hotels like the Hotel Metropole in Blackpool, Lancashire.

The first public parks

From 1840 onwards, many towns opened parks. The first, in Derby, was provided by Joseph Strutt, a local textile mill owner, as a space for his workers to enjoy some fresh air. It was free to visit the park on Wednesdays and Sundays. Many parks had bandstands, where people could sit and listen to a brass band playing in the evenings and on Sundays during the summer.

Bandstand in the park, Beamish Open-Air Museum, County Durham

Other popular entertainments included going to the music hall (although this was regarded as rather lower-class) and pantomimes. By the end of Victoria's reign, people were watching lantern shows, often of distant parts of the Empire, and from 1894 the first silent moving pictures began to be shown in early cinemas.

A women's final tennis match at the old Wimbledon, 1905

Sport

The railways helped the growth of professional sport. It was now possible for teams to travel long distances to play each other. In 1872, the first ever FA Cup Final was attended by 2000 people. In cricket, the first test match between England and Australia was held in Melbourne in 1877. W. G. Grace was by far the most famous cricketer of the time, and helped to make cricket a popular spectator sport. Also in 1877, the first tennis tournament was held at Wimbledon. Cycling became popular too, both as something to do and as a sport to watch, although many people were shocked when women wore shorts or trousers to cycle.

> The first ever FA Cup Final was in 1872, when Wanderers beat Royal Engineers 1–0.

Think about it!

1. Which people could afford to go out for entertainment in Victorian times?
2. How important was the railway in leisure activities?
3. Why were people so shocked about women cyclists?

Let's do it!

1. What can you learn about the Victorian seaside from the image of the Hotel Metropole?
2. Which kind of people would stay at the hotel?
3. Why did sport become so popular in the 1870s?

As homes were so crowded, most children spent their free time in the street. There wasn't much traffic, except on busy town centre streets, so it was safer to play outside. Don't forget that, until 1871, when education was made **compulsory**, many children worked full- or part-time.

Street entertainment

A barrel organ and pet monkey entertain on the streets

Travelling entertainers would tour the streets. One of the best liked was the barrel organ, which could play popular tunes of the day by turning a handle. The organ was often accompanied by a pet monkey, who might be trained to pass around the hat to collect pennies from the children. A barrel organ would quickly attract a crowd of children and have them dancing in the street.

Skipping was very popular

Games

Boys would play cricket and football in the street – if they couldn't afford a ball, they would make one out of old rags. Marbles, roller-skates, spinning tops, skipping ropes, hoop and stick and yo-yos were all popular for those who could afford them. Indoor games included dolls, tea sets, toy soldiers and theatres, as well as reading, although most books had few

W. CROYDON. PHOTO.   94. CORNWALL RP

> Why might the barrel-organ owner have a pet monkey with them?

(if any) pictures and the printing was very small.

Travelling fairs

Probably the highlight of the year would be the arrival of the travelling fair. Even if you had no money, you could still watch everything. Children would try to save up for weeks and weeks so they had a few pennies to spend at the fair! There would be swings, rides powered by steam engines, coconut

Victorian fair at the Black Country Museum

shies, shooting galleries, all accompanied by loud music and lit up at night by bright lights. What a contrast this would be to the normally drab towns and cities. The fairs also had food stalls selling sweets and roasted chestnuts, and strongmen, jugglers and fortune-tellers wandering around the fair.

Special treats

Sometimes, organisations like Dr Barnardo's would arrange special treats and outings for children from the cities so they could spend a day in the country or at the seaside. A picnic would be provided for everyone. Many Victorians thought it was very important that children had some fresh air away from the dirt, smell and noise of the cities.

Think about it!

1. How similar were Victorian entertainments to those we have today?
2. Do you think *all* Victorian children had fun?
3. Why do you think some Victorians thought it was important for children to spend time in the countryside?

Let's do it!

1. Find out how a barrel organ works.
2. Imagine you have been to the travelling fair. Write a letter to a friend who could not be there.
3. Who had more fun in the Victorian period – adults or children?

Key word

compulsory

Photograph showing part of Buffalo Bill's Wild West Show, 1890. Which one in the photo is Buffalo Bill?

The Victorians loved the **exotic**, and that is why zoos and circuses were very popular. Remember: in 1850, most of Africa was still unknown to Europeans and labelled as 'unexplored' on the map.

Buffalo Bill

William Cody was born in 1846 in the Wild West. He worked as a scout for the army, a buffalo hunter supplying fresh meat for railway workers, and served in the army during the American Civil War. In 1869, a book telling his story became a best seller in the USA. In 1883, he set up his Wild West Show, which toured across America each summer. In 1887, he brought his show to Europe, including London. He performed a private show for Queen Victoria, who liked it so much she asked for another one to entertain her Golden Jubilee guests. The show was a great success. There were 300 performances, which sold over 2.5 million tickets. Each show lasted for three to four hours. The show featured cowboys, Native Americans, hunting scenes using real animals like buffalo and deer, rodeo stunts, sharp shooting and re-enactments of real events, like the death of General Custer at the Battle of the Little Bighorn. The public loved it!

Circuses

Circuses originally performed in the open air, but by 1850 most of the Victorian circuses were performing in a tent or 'big top'. By 1890, some of these could seat 7000 people! Music halls and theatres also included circus performers in their shows. Circuses would announce their arrival in a town or city with a big parade of all the performers and animals, and people would come from far away just to see the parade, which might be 5 kilometres long. Often, circuses would also feature a '**freak show**' showing off human **curiosities** like the 'Bearded Lady' or the 'Smallest [or Tallest] Man in the World', the 'Tattooed Man', or perhaps even a **cannibal** from the Pacific Ocean.

> Victorians loved going to the circus – it was a rare opportunity to see exotic animals from other countries.

A Victorian circus poster

Think about it!

1. Look carefully at the circus poster. What do you think was the attraction of a visit to the circus?
2. What do Buffalo Bill's Wild West Show and a Victorian circus have in common?
3. What was the appeal of 'freak shows'?
4. How similar were Victorian circuses to those we visit today?

Let's do it!

1. This unit has looked at how the Victorians had fun. You have discovered a lot of evidence about leisure activities. Now we want you to use that evidence to answer the question 'Did the Victorians have fun in their spare time?'
2. Which evidence will you use? Which will you ignore? Is all the evidence equally useful? Think carefully before you write.

Key words

exotic   freak show   curiosities   cannibal

Today, everyone over the age of 18 can vote in elections to choose the government that runs Britain. The Prime Minister runs the country because more people voted for their party than for any other party. If we don't like what they do, then we can vote for someone else in the next election. Everybody over the age of 18 can be involved in deciding who runs the country in Britain. But it wasn't always like this.

The Chartists

When Victoria became Queen, only about 450,000 men could vote, and no women at all. These men were rich, and controlled the country – and they were not keen to give up power to the rest of the population. In the 1830s and 1840s, thousands of people joined together to support an organisation called the Chartists. They wanted everybody to be able to vote. They thought if everyone could vote, then life would be fairer – wages would go up, and living and working conditions would get

> When Queen Victoria came to the throne, only one in seven men – and no women – could vote to choose the government.

Photograph of a Chartist Meeting, 1848

better, because people would only vote for someone who promised to help them to get a better life. The Government did not like this idea. Some Chartists were sent to prison, and others were transported to Australia. The Chartists failed to get their way.

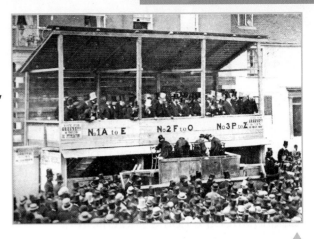

Voting in an election, 1860s

More people can vote

Gradually the idea grew that it was a good idea if more people took part in elections to choose governments. In 1867, more men were given the vote (33 per cent of adult males could now vote) and, in 1884, some working men were given the vote. By now 66 per cent of all men could choose the government. Voting was done at a large public meeting, so everyone knew how you voted. It was quite common, for example, to lose your job if you voted against your employer's wishes. In 1872, the secret ballot was introduced, so nobody would know how you voted. Slowly, Britain's Government was becoming more democratic.

Democracy was invented by the Ancient Greeks in Athens around 500 BCE, when adult men met to take decisions on running the city. It was slowly being introduced in Queen Victoria's Britain.

Think about it!

1. Why did the Chartists want everyone to have the vote?
2. Why did the Government oppose that idea?
3. How democratic was Britain by the 1880s?

Key words

democracy

hustings

Let's do it!

1. Find out how Britain's Government works. How is it elected? How often are elections? Who decides what the Government will do?

2. Research the Chartists. The Chartists had *six* demands about how Parliament should work, five of which apply today. If the Charter was such a good idea, why was it opposed by the Government?

3. Imagine you are going to vote in an election at the **hustings** in the photo above. Describe the scene. How would you feel? What would you do?

In the house

Most Victorians believed that men and women were different. They thought that men were best suited to work, the army and politics. Women's job was looking after the home and children. Rich women had lots of servants to run the home for them. Poor women had to work *and* also look after the house and children. When Queen Victoria came to the throne, women could not own a house or have legal control of their own children. Everything was organised either by their fathers or, once they married, their husbands.

Cartoon from 1842 showing a Victorian view of women

Education

Girls were educated differently to boys. Rich girls were taught at home. They were expected to be able to sing and play the piano, sew, make polite conversation,

perhaps learn French or Italian. But, most importantly, girls were taught to run the home. In 1851, Mrs Beeton published her famous *Book of Household Management*, which contained recipes but also tips on how to keep the house running smoothly. In 1840, over 60 per cent of women were **illiterate**, but gradually schools for girls opened and some girls even went to university. After 1870, poor girls might be taught to read and write, but also to cook and clean, as many

Page from Mrs Beeton's book, showing some of the dishes she cooked. Do you think her book was aimed at rich people or poor people?

of them would end up working as servants.

Women get more control over their lives

Several changes were made during the 19th century. Women were given control of their children, they could divorce husbands who behaved badly to them (but this cost a great deal of money and was very difficult), and in 1884 they could own property and keep control of their own money. Yet they still could not vote.

▲ *Women demanding the vote*

When Queen Victoria died, women still *could not vote in elections.*

Votes for women

The Manchester Society for Women's Suffrage was set up in 1867 to try to get women the vote, but this was refused. From then on there were many protests aimed at changing the law. In 1897, the National Union of Women's Suffrage Societies (NUWSS) was set up, uniting all the different groups working to get women the vote, but many people – men and women – opposed the idea. Queen Victoria and Florence Nightingale were just two famous women who opposed women getting the vote. However, many other women, like men, thought their lives would be much better if they could vote too.

Think about it!

1. What kind of education do you think the 'Accomplished Young Lady' in the cartoon at the top of page 40 has had? What do you think is her main aim in life?
2. Why were women educated differently to men?
3. Why did women want the vote?

Key word

illiterate

Let's do it!

1. Find out about some of the women who were involved in the campaigns to change the lives of women in Victorian times. Why did they want change?
2. When did women in Britain get the vote? Has getting the vote made any difference to the lives of women?

7.3 What about the workers? How did their lives get better?

Stopping work to get better conditions

Matchgirls worked 70 hours a week making matches in London and earned 5 shillings (25p) a week. The work involved dipping small sticks into a mixture containing phosphorus. The work was dangerous – quite often they would get '**phossy jaw**', which made the flesh fall off their faces and gave them brain tumours. Of course, there was no sick pay like there is in Britain today. Eventually the workers had had enough. Led by Annie Besant, a lady who believed everyone should have a decent wage and good working conditions, the matchgirls went on strike for five weeks. Eventually their employers, Bryant & May, gave in and agreed to introduce better working conditions and increase pay. It was the first ever successful strike by women in Britain.

Protest march during the matchgirls' strike, 1888

If you were too sick to work, you didn't get paid.

The London Dock Strike, 1889

Every morning, around 12,000 labourers turned up at the gates of the London Docks, hoping for work loading or unloading ships. Only 5000 of them might get some work. They might be employed for the day, for half a day or for a couple of hours. They were only paid for the hours they worked, so they might stand around outside the docks for half a day before earning anything. On average, they were paid 4d (not even 2p) per hour. Many were lucky to get work for three hours a day.

In 1889, partly inspired by the matchgirls, they stopped work. They demanded a minimum of half a day's pay each day, and to be paid at 6d (2.5p) an hour. The dock owners refused their demands, so the dockworkers stayed away from work for over five weeks. Food was rotting on the ships, shops were running out of supplies, people were getting angry. Finally, the dock owners gave in. They agreed to pay 6d (2.5p) an hour. Ordinary people were doing something for themselves to help improve their lives.

▲ Dockworkers trying to get a day's work, London, 1889

Think about it!

1. Why did the matchgirls of Bryant & May stop work? Why were they successful?
2. Why did the London Dock labourers go on strike? Why were they successful?
3. The Chartists (see Unit 7.1) thought that, if they got the vote, life would be better. Did the matchgirls and the London dockworkers feel the same way?
4. Which was the best way to improve pay and living conditions – voting in Parliament or stopping working?

Let's do it!

1. More and more people could vote and take part in government during Victorian times. Britain was becoming more democratic.

   Find out about democracy in Ancient Greece. It was first introduced in Athens around 500 BCE. Compare Greek democracy with democracy in Victorian Britain. How similar are they?

Key word

phossy jaw

A murderer is caught!

'A murderer has just been committed at Salt Hill and the suspected murderer was seen to take a first class ticket to London by the train which left Slough at 7:42 p.m. He is in the garb of a **Quaker** with a great coat on which reaches nearly down to his feet. He is in the last compartment of the second class compartment.'

▲ John Tawell at his trial, drawn by someone in court

John Tawell went to Slough on 1 January 1845, to see his friend. He killed her by putting poison in the drink he gave her. He was seen leaving the murder scene and was followed to Slough railway station, where he got a train to London. The stationmaster sent a telegraph to the police at Paddington station. When the train arrived, Tawell was arrested. He was later found guilty of murder and executed in front of 10,000 people. If it was not for the telegraph, he would have escaped!

The Penny Post

Before 1840, few people sent letters. Post was very expensive – it might cost at least one shilling (5p) to receive a letter and the recipient didn't know what was in it. All this changed in 1840, when the Penny Post was introduced. A letter could be sent anywhere in the country for just 1d (less than 0.5p). The first postage stamp in the world was the famous Penny Black. Soon, the distinctive red postboxes could be seen all over the country. People began to write to each other much more, and before long celebration cards were sent in huge numbers, as well as picture postcards from the seaside. You could send a letter and it would quickly be delivered anywhere in the country.

Before 1840, you paid for a letter when you received it.

◀ *A Victorian postbox. How can you tell it is Victorian?*

Replica Victorian telephone. Can you figure out how it works? ▶

Other inventions

Towards the end of Queen Victoria's reign, other inventions made communications speedier, but they were not widely used until the 20th century. The typewriter, telephone and telegram delivery service were all introduced, helping businesses to grow and people to keep in touch with each other much better.

Think about it!

1. Was John Tawell unlucky to be caught?
2. Why was the Penny Post so successful?
3. Which of the changes to communication do you think was most important? Why?

Let's do it!

1. Find out about the telegraph. When was it invented? How did it work?
2. What is a Quaker? What do they believe in? Does that make the murder of John Tawell's friend even more shocking?
3. How do we communicate today? Is it similar or different to Victorian times?

Key word

Quaker

We have already seen how unhealthy the towns and cities were, but gradually they became healthier places to live.

Preventing disease

Edward Jenner had discovered how to prevent **smallpox**. In 1840, the Government made **immunisation** free for children and, in 1853, they were made compulsory. Deaths from smallpox fell from 300 per million people to around 20 per million. John Snow worked out that **cholera**, another killer disease, was caused by dirty water and then, in 1892, a vaccine was discovered. Another major disease was being controlled. New sewers were built under the streets of London and other cities to clean up the towns. Public Health Acts made it compulsory for towns to improve living conditions.

DEATH'S DISPENSARY.
OPEN TO THE POOR, GRATIS, BY PERMISSION OF THE PARISH.

Cartoon from 1866 suggesting disease is caused by dirty water collected from a hand pump. Few houses had their own water supply at this time

Hospitals and nursing

In 1837, hospitals were places people went to die. Hospital buildings were dirty, medical care was poor and nurses were often untrained. Nursing was not seen as a job for a respectable woman. One person changed all that. Florence Nightingale improved the hospitals for wounded soldiers during the Crimean War. When she returned to England, she set up a school to train nurses, and set about improving hospitals, making them clean and airy and offering better medical care. Soon after this, X-rays were invented, so it was easier to find out

An operation in progress in the 1920s

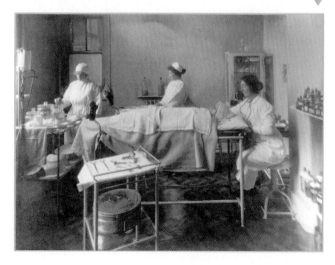

what was wrong with a patient. If you were sick, you now had a much better chance of surviving.

Having an operation

Having an operation in the 1840s was very dangerous – about half of all patients died, usually from infection caught during the operation or from shock caused by the pain. Things changed as doctors started to use **anaesthetics** to send the patient to sleep, which reduced the risk of shock. Queen Victoria used anaesthetics when she was having a baby, so suddenly it became very popular. **Antiseptics** were discovered and used to keep wounds clean and prevent infection. By 1900, many more people were surviving quite complicated operations.

The discovery of anaesthetics and antiseptic made operations much safer.

Think about it!

1. What do you think was the biggest change in medicine and health? Why?
2. Was it safer having an operation in 1900 than in 1800? Why?
3. Were towns better places to live by 1901?

Ian Dawson, an historian and history teacher, believes someone is significant if he/she:

- changed events at the time they lived
- improved lots of people's lives – or made them worse
- changed people's ideas
- had a long-lasting impact on their country or the world
- had been a really good or a very bad example to other people on how to live or behave.

Let's do it!

1. Research the improvements to nursing and hospitals made by Florence Nightingale.
2. How significant a person was Florence Nightingale?
3. Do the improvements in health and medicine suggest that the Victorians were very clever?

Key words

smallpox   immunisation   cholera   anaesthetics   antiseptics

Even more inventions

We have already seen how railways and steamships completely changed life in Victorian times, but there were plenty of other important inventions. Electricity, the sewing machine and vacuum cleaner were Victorian inventions, even if they were not widely used until later. The first aeroplane flew in America shortly after Queen Victoria died. Charles Babbage invented the 'difference engine', which carried out large mathematical calculations and was the beginning of the development of computers. The first moving (but silent) pictures were invented, and early cinemas were very popular.

> *The Victorian period was a time when people used science to try to improve everyday life for millions of people.*

Think about it!

1. How important was science in Victorian times?
2. How did it help to make life better for people?

Controversy

In 1859, Charles Darwin published his famous book *On the Origin of Species*, about the evolution of man and claiming humans were descended from apes. His book caused huge controversy at the time. Many Christian people believed that man was created by God and so Darwin could not possibly be right. His ideas are still argued over today.

Charles Darwin, like many other Victorians, believed in science. He thought that by observing things, and carrying out careful experiments, you could discover things about life and make it better. Victorian times are the first time in history that many, many people used science to try to improve everyday life for millions of people.

Picture of Charles Darwin, drawn in 1871, making fun of his theory of evolution ▼

Let's do it!

One of the most important skills in history is to be able to construct an argument and make it convincing by using evidence to support your argument. At the start of this book we suggested that most people in Victorian Britain were poor and lived in horrible conditions. Many of the units are headed 'Change(s) in...' Historians talk about the Victorian times as the 'great changes'. You should by now be in a position to decide for yourself whether there were great changes or not.

We would like you to answer the question 'Did life get better for everybody during Queen Victoria's reign?'

1. To do this successfully, you need to sort your ideas into two sections: 'Life did get better' and "Life didn't get better'.

2. Next, you need to structure your ideas to make the best argument you can.

3. Finally, you need to reach a conclusion.

Have fun!

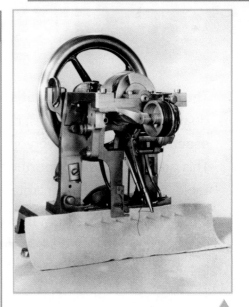

A Victorian sewing machine

Skills grid

Unit	Skills
1	sense of period, significant individual and event
2	continuity and change
3	cause and consequence
4	similarity and difference
5	continuity and change, interpretations
6	using evidence to reach a conclusion
7	making a comparison between units [Ancient Greece and Britain]
8	presenting a clear and convincing argument

The Victorians gathered **statistics** all the time. They recorded births, marriages and deaths; population of cities; numbers of people emigrating to other countries; and especially the census. Everyone in the country was counted every 10 years from 1801. This gives us a great opportunity to combine history and maths. The census is just one big table, waiting to be interpreted!

Obviously one page from the census gives a limited data set, but it is enough to be useful. Starter questions might include:

- How many people live in these five houses?
- Who is the oldest?
- Who is the youngest?
- How many are male? How many are female?

> A census is taken every 10 years and counts all the people living in Britain.

Page from the 1881 census, for the village of Renhold, Bedfordshire

No. of Schedule	ROAD, STREET, &c. and No. or NAME of HOUSE	HOUSES Inhabited	HOUSES Uninhabited (U.), or Building (B.)	NAME and Surname of each Person	RELATION to Head of Family	CONDITION as to Marriage	AGE last Birthday of Males	AGE last Birthday of Females	Rank, Profession, or OCCUPATION	WHERE BORN
28	Church Houses	1		Henry Gurney	Head	Mar:	59		Ag: Lab:	Beds - Renhold
				Sarah. do	Wife	Mar		54	Lace Maker	Beds - Great Barford
				Albert. do	Son	Unm:	23		Ag: Lab:	Beds - Renhold
				Alma. I. do	Son	Unm	21		Ag: Lab.	Do. Do
				William. do	Son	Unm:	16		Ag: Lab	Do Do
				Laura. A. do	Granddaughter	Unm:		12	Lace Maker	Do Do
29	Church House	1		John Sharp	Head	Mar:	79		Ag: Lab.	Do Do
				Eliza. do	Wife	Mar		80	Lace Maker	Beds: Willington
30	Church House	1		David Dawson	Head	Mar:	76		Ag: Lab.	Beds - Renhold
				Elizabeth. do	Wife	Mar:		75	Sempstress	Huntingdonsh: Upton.
				John. do	Son	Unm:	35		Ag: Lab	Beds - Renhold
				Letitia. do	Daur:	Unm:		31	Lace Maker	Do Do
31	Church House	1		Abraham Sletcher	Head	Mar:	28		Brick Maker	Do Do
				Matilda do	Wife	Mar:		27	Lace Maker	Do Do
				Hannah. M: do	Daur:			11	Scholar	Do Do
				Ada. I. do	Daur:			7	Scholar	Do Do
				James. F. do	Son		4			Do Do
	The Church									
32	The Vicarage	1		Josiah Spencer	Head	Mar:	64		Vicar of Renhold	Surry - Hampstead Park
				Philadelphia R. do	Wife	Mar:		59		Bucks: High Wycombe
				Dora Leigh do	Daur:	Unm:		23		Herts - Harpenden
				Maude Leigh. do	Daur:	Unm:		20		Beds - Renhold
				Martha Trusham	Servant	Unm:		45	Parlour Maid Domestic Servant	Herts - Montpelier
				Laura. M. Jones	Servant	Unm:		33	Cook Domestic Servant	Gloucestersh: Hatherley
				Emily. C. Hope	Servant	Unm:		16	Housemaid Domestic Servant	Middlesex: Paddington
	Total of Houses	5				Total of Males and Females...	10	14		

- How many different jobs can you find?
- Which is the largest family?
- Which is the smallest family?
- How many people were born in Renhold?
- How many people were born in Bedfordshire? How many were born outside of Bedfordshire? You might turn these numbers into percentages!

All these questions are designed to help extract information from the census, and to form a basis for asking important historical questions about the Victorian countryside. We're sure you can think of many more questions to ask.

Think about it!

1. Unit 2 looked at life in the countryside. Look back at the work you did there. How much does the census data agree with what you found out in Unit 2? How much does it disagree?

Let's do it!

1. Construct an age pyramid for these 25 people. What does it tell us about Victorian country life?

2. Where were people born? How far have most people travelled in their life? Look at the vicar. How many different places has he lived in with his family? How can you tell? (Clue: look at the 'Where born' column.)

3. How can we tell that there was a school in the village? Going to school was made compulsory in 1870.

4. Which family had servants? What jobs did the servants do? What does that tell us about life in Victorian Britain?

You can carry out similar mathematical and historical activities using any of the sets of data collected by the Victorians that you can research. Have fun!

Key word

statistics

Technology had a huge impact on the lives of Victorians, whether they lived in the countryside or in the towns and cities, whether they worked in agriculture or industry. Technology made towns safer places to live (sewers); made surgery safer (anaesthetics and antiseptics); made food cheaper (McCormick's reaper and refrigerated transport bringing frozen meat halfway across the world); made communications and travel much quicker (telegraph, railway and steamship); and made industrial production much faster and cheaper (steam engine and power looms in cotton factories). Looking at the Victorians helps us to understand how key events and individuals in design and technology have helped to shape the world we live in.

Key individuals

Perhaps the greatest individual engineer of Victorian times, Isambard Kingdom Brunel is famous for his work on railways, and in building steamships, bridges and docks. Can you imagine the Victorian world without his contributions? Not content to build a railway from London to Bristol, he had a vision of luxury ships taking passengers on to New York and the New World. Even people at the time thought of him as a genius, an icon of engineering, and the image of progress and prosperity. He died in 1859, at the age of 53, from overwork and exhaustion.

Isambard Kingdom Brunel
▼

Think about it!

1. What, in your opinion, was Isambard Kingdom Brunel's greatest contribution to Victorian progress?

2. In what ways has Brunel helped shape the world we live in today?

Key events

In Unit 1 you found out about the Great Exhibition of 1851, which was designed to show off the new technologies of Victorian Britain. The building itself was innovative – Paxton's Crystal Palace was made from over 300,000 sheets of glass. The 100,000 exhibits, showing the best in modern technology from across the world, were seen by millions, helped by the railway and Thomas Cook's cheap trains to London. Isn't that an example of a key event that helped to shape the world we live in?

The Great Exhibition of 1851

We're sure you can think of many more key events and individuals from the work you have done on the Victorians. Which people and events are at the top of *your* list?

Let's do it!

1. Use a table like this one to draw up a list of key events and people from Victorian times that have helped to shape the world we live in. You might need to do some more research, or you can use the people and events in this book.

Individual	Event

2. Next, prioritise each list, with the one you think is most important at the top, and the least important at the bottom.

3. Finally, choose *one* person and *one* event that, in your opinion, has had the most important influence on the way we live today. Remember to explain what that person did and what that event was.

4. Discuss with others in your group and find out if their lists are the same as yours.

Ancient Greece

3000 BCE   2000 BCE   1000 BCE

Ancient Egypt

School is made compulsory!

In 1870, something happened that had never happened before in Britain – all children, from the age of 5 to 10, had to go to school. In 1880, schools were made free and, in 1893, the school leaving age was increased to 11. Of course, *some* children had gone to school before 1870, especially rich children, but it had never been compulsory. Rich boys often went to boarding schools, where they were taught all the skills necessary to run the Empire. Rich girls usually had a **governess**, who taught them at home.

Inside a Victorian school classroom

What did children study?

Mostly the 3Rs – reading, writing and arithmetic, with emphasis on physical education as well (the Victorians called it 'drill'). Girls and boys were taught together in the youngest classes, but older pupils were separated. Boys were taught practical subjects, and girls learned to sew and cook, to help them get a job. Later, geography, history and science were added to the curriculum.

In a Tudor classroom

School in Tudor times

As a boy, William Shakespeare attended a grammar school in Stratford-upon-Avon. There, he learned to read and write, as well as studying Greek and Latin. His father was wealthy enough to be able to pay for him to go to school. Most boys worked, helping their father and learning his trade. Girls would be taught at home the skills needed to run a household.

Tudors

| 0 | 1000 CE | | 2000 CE |

Ancient Rome

Victorian times

Roman, Greek and Egyptian schools

In Roman and Greek times, only the sons of the rich went to school. A Greek boy would be accompanied to school by a slave, who would carry his work. In Egypt, a boy would learn from his father, so a stonemason would teach his son to be a stonemason, and a scribe would teach his son to read and write. Remember: in Egypt, Greece and Rome, few people could read and write.

▲ *Learning to write in Ancient Greece*

Think about it!

1. Why do you think schooling was made compulsory in Victorian Britain in 1870?

2. Is this a photograph of a younger class or an older class? How can you tell?

3. How similar were Tudor and Ancient Greek schools to Victorian schools?

4. How similar are these to the school you are in today?

Let's do it!

1. Research how schools and schooling have changed throughout history. Some questions you might consider:

   - Who went to school?

   - What were they taught?

   - How strict were schools – what happened if you misbehaved?

   - Did pupils wear uniform?

   - What did they write on?

2. You can probably think of many more. Present your findings, with the heading 'Schools through the ages'.

3. When would you have rather gone to school? Why?

Key word

governess

Historians often call the Victorian period a time of 'great changes'. You have been studying the Victorian period, so should be able to decide for yourself whether you agree with this or not.

Do you think Victorian times should be called the 'great changes'?

Think about it!

1. Review your work on the Victorian period and make a list of all the changes you have studied. Your list might include railways, factories, the growth of cities, going to school, and many, many, more.

2. Sort your list into three columns: 'Big changes', 'Medium changes' and 'Small changes'.

3. Looking at the 'Big changes', do you think that the Victorian period deserves to be known as the 'great changes'? Why?

The last 50 years

Think about changes in society in the last 50 years. How many changes can you come up with? Here are some to help you get started:

There are many more changes you might have thought of for yourself. But how about the status and role of women? Human rights? Electric cars? Solar panels and renewable energy? Or MRI scans? Medical care and organ transplants? Globalisation and the spread of global brands like McDonald's and Starbucks? Microwave ovens, fridges and freezers? Instant television coverage of events all over the world? Twenty-four-hour news channels? Again, sort your list into three columns: 'Big changes', 'Medium changes' and 'Small changes'. Which are the most important changes you have come up with?

A satellite in space. In what ways do we rely on satellites in everyday life? ▼

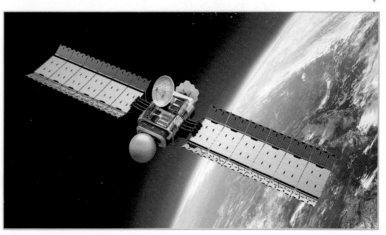

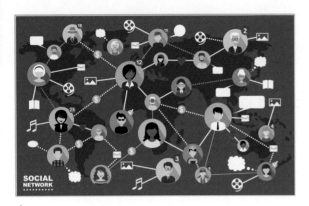

The internet connecting people around the world. How did we communicate with other people before the World Wide Web was developed?

An early mobile phone. What do we use mobile phones for today? Are they just used for making telephone calls?

Let's do it!

1. Research change in the last 50 years. You could stick with our suggestions, although you will be able to come up with many more yourself. In what ways have these changes altered the way we live?

2. How similar is our life today to that of our parents growing up? Talk to your parents and ask them what *they* think are the biggest changes. Is their list of big changes the same as yours? What do the two lists tell us about change in the last 50 years?

Pulling it all together

In your opinion, do the changes in the last 50 years or so add up to a time of 'great changes'? Have all these changes had a big impact on the way we live our lives? What has been the biggest impact, do you think? If the Victorian period is known as the 'great changes', what would you call the last 50 years?

Finally, compare the changes in Victorian times with the changes over the last 50 years. Which period changed the most? Which changed the fastest? Which changed to the benefit of most people?

Glossary

Abdicate: stop ruling a country, give up being king or queen

Acts: new laws

Anaesthetics: put a patient to sleep making an operation safer

Antiseptics: prevent infection of a cut

Assassinate: kill

Biographers: authors who write someone's life story

Broth: a soup made of meat or vegetables cooked in stock

Cannibal: someone who eats human flesh

Census: counting everyone who lives in the country

Cholera: killer disease caused by dirty infected water

Clippers: special fast sailing ships designed for long journeys

Coaster: small ship carrying goods, doesn't travel far from land

Colony: country controlled by another, part of an empire

Communally: together, agreeing what to do

Commuter: someone who travels to work every day

Compensation: payment for causing an injury

Compulsory: something you have to do, have no choice about

Coronation: special event making a person king or queen of a country

Curiosities: special interests

Democracy: where everyone can choose the government

Domestic system: making things, like wool, at home on a small scale

Emigrated: went to live and work in another country

Empire: where one country controls and rules lots of other countries

Exotic: unusual, different, from somewhere hardly known

Freak show: a show of unusual exhibits

Governess: female teacher employed specially to teach one person at home

Hustings: open-air voting, where everyone can see and hear what is going on

Illiterate: can't read or write

Immunisation: injection to prevent disease

Innovation: new

Irregular: from time to time, not full time

Live in: have a room or bed in the house of the farmer who employed them

Mechanisation: when machines are included in a process

Merchant navy: ships that carry goods, not fighting ships

Missionaries: religious people who go to other countries to try to persuade the people who live there to be religious too

Navvies: workers

Phossy jaw: disease that affects skin and bone

Poach: steal

Prefabricated: made in a factory and taken to a site to put together

Quaker: a religious group which believes in quiet prayer

Reprisals: acts of revenge

Sepoys: Indian soldiers in the British army in India

Smallpox: very infectious disease that killed thousands of people in Victorian times

Stationary engine: steam engine that is fixed in one place, that can't move, that has no wheels

Statistics: keeping records, collecting data

Suburbs: parts of a town or city that are away from the centre

Traction engines: vehicles used to pull heavy loads

Trade union: organisation where workers join together to try to improve their working lives and wages

Transported: sent to another country as a prisoner, to work, as a punishment

Unadulterated: not had other things added to it

Water closets: flushing toilets

Index

World map

North Pole

GREENLAND

ICELAND

NORW

UNITED
KINGDOM DENM

IRELAND

CANADA

GERM
AL
C

FRANCE

SPAIN

PORTUGAL

MOROCCO

UNITED STATES
OF AMERICA

ALGERIA

MEXICO

CUBA

MAURITANIA

MALI

NIGE

JAMAICA

SENEGAL

GUATEMALA

NICARAGUA

GUINEA

NIGERI

COSTA RICA

VENEZUELA

PANAMA

GHANA

COLOMBIA

GUYANA

ATLANTIC
OCEAN

Equator

ECUADOR

GABON

PERU

BRAZIL

PACIFIC
OCEAN

BOLIVIA

PARAGUAY

CHILE

N

URUGUAY

ARGENTINA

SOUTHERN C

South Pole

ARCTIC OCEAN

RUSSIA

KAZAKHSTAN

MONGOLIA

AINE

TURKEY   TURKMENISTAN

SYRIA   AFGHANISTAN

RAEL   IRAQ
JORDAN   IRAN   PAKISTAN   NEPAL

GYPT   SAUDI
        ARABIA   INDIA   MYANMAR

        OMAN

UDAN   THAILAND
    ERITREA YEMEN   VIETNAM

SOUTH   ETHIOPIA   SRI
SUDAN   LANKA

        SOMALIA

KENYA

TIC
OF
GO

    TANZANIA

BIA

MOZAMBIQUE

MADAGASCAR

JAPAN

CHINA

PACIFIC
OCEAN

PHILIPPINES

MALAYSIA

Equator

INDONESIA   PAPUA NEW
                GUINEA

INDIAN

OCEAN   SOLOMON
                            ISLANDS

                        VANUATU

            AUSTRALIA

                NEW
                ZEALAND

63

Acknowledgements

The publishers wish to thank the following for permission to reproduce images. Every effort has been made to trace copyright holders and to obtain their permission for the use of copyright materials. The publishers will gladly receive any information enabling them to rectify any error or omission at the first opportunity.

(t = top, c = centre, b = bottom, r = right, l = left)

p4 The Royal Family in 1846 (oil on canvas), Winterhalter, Franz Xaver (1805-73)/Royal Collection Trust © Her Majesty Queen Elizabeth II, 2019/Bridgeman Images; p5 Everett Historical/Shutterstock; p6 GL Archive/Alamy Stock Photo; p7 IanDagnall Computing/Alamy Stock Photo; p8 Pictorial Press Ltd/Alamy Stock Photo; p9 Amoret Tanner/Alamy Stock Photo; p10 Ivy Close Images/Alamy Stock Photo; p11l Ajax News & Feature Service/Alamy Stock Photo; p11r Milkmaids, 1857 (gold-toned albumen print), Hemphill, William Despard (1816-1902)/Sean Sexton Collection/ Bridgeman Images; p12t World History Archive/Alamy Stock Photo; p12b Chronicle/Alamy Stock Photo; p14 Granger Historical Picture Archive/Alamy Stock Photo; p15l © Museum of London; p15r Ros Crosland/Alamy Stock Photo; p16 Print Collector/Contributor/Getty Images; p17l ©Alf Wilkinson; p17r Universal History Archive/Contributor/ Getty Images; p18 Public domain via British Library; p19l Historic Images/Alamy Stock Photo; p19r Pictorial Press Ltd/ Alamy Stock Photo; p20t Chronicle/Alamy Stock Photo; p20b Science & Society Picture Library/Contributor/Getty Images; p21 Chronicle/Alamy Stock Photo; p22t SOTK2011/Alamy Stock Photo; p22b Igor Golovnov/Alamy Stock Photo; p23 Lordprice Collection/Alamy Stock Photo; p24t Chronicle/Alamy Stock Photo; p24b Wolverhampton City Council - Arts and Heritage/Alamy Stock Photo; p25 Chronicle/Alamy Stock Photo; p27 CH Collection/Alamy Stock Photo; p28 Iconographic Archive/Alamy Stock Photo; p29 Mazur Travel/Shutterstock; p30 Public domain; p31 Pictorial Press Ltd/Alamy Stock Photo; p32t Heritage Image Partnership Ltd/Alamy Stock Photo; p32b ©Alf Wilkinson; p33 The Print Collector/Alamy Stock Photo; p34t KGPA Ltd/Alamy Stock Photo; p34b Chronicle/Alamy Stock Photo; p35 ©Alf Wilkinson; p36 The Protected Art Archive/Alamy Stock Photo; p37 The Artchives/Alamy Stock Photo; p38 The Picture Art Collection/Alamy Stock Photo; p39 Public domain; p40t Punch Cartoon Library/TopFoto; p40b Shawshots/Alamy Stock Photo; p41 Archive Pics/Alamy Stock Photo; p42 World History Archive/Alamy Stock Photo; p43 Artokoloro Quint Lox Limited/Alamy Stock Photo; p44 Artokoloro Quint Lox Limited/Alamy Stock Photo; p45l Paul Martin/Alamy Stock Photo; p45r Roger Cracknell 01/classic /Alamy Stock Photo; p46t Science History Images/Alamy Stock Photo; p46b thislife pictures/Alamy Stock Photo; p48 Classic Image/Alamy Stock Photo; p49 Granger Historical Picture Archive/ Alamy Stock Photo; p50 Public domain; p52 Pictorial Press Ltd/Alamy Stock Photo; p53 Chronicle/Alamy Stock Photo; p54t thislife pictures/Alamy Stock Photo; p54b The Wonderful Story of Britain: At School in Tudor Times, Jackson, Peter (1922-2003)/Private Collection/© Look and Learn/Bridgeman Images; p55 Egyptian scribe and Greek schoolboy (litho), English School, (20th century)/Private Collection/Look and Learn/Elgar Collection/Bridgeman Images; p56 NASA; p57l Gurza/Shutterstock; p57r Chris Willson/Alamy Stock Photo.